LINCOLN CASTLE

THE MEDIEVAL STORY

The common seal of the city of Lincoln,
representing a castle with
city shield of arms over the gate.

The title page gives an alternative view of the gatehouse with, tall
conical roofs to the towers, copied from the common seal of the city.
There is no evidence to prove that the castle on the seal was Lincoln
Castle, but the striking similarity between the two buildings makes
it seem likely.

LINCOLN CASTLE

THE MEDIEVAL STORY

Sheila Sancha

LINCOLNSHIRE COUNTY COUNCIL
Recreational Services : Tourism

Published by Lincolnshire County Council : Recreational Services — Tourism

© 1985 Sheila Sancha

First Published 1985

ISBN 0 86111 121 4

Printed by High Resolution Graphics Limited, Grimsby.

Books by the same author:

Knight After Knight — Collins
The Castle Story — Kestrel and Penguin Books
The Luttrell Village — Collins

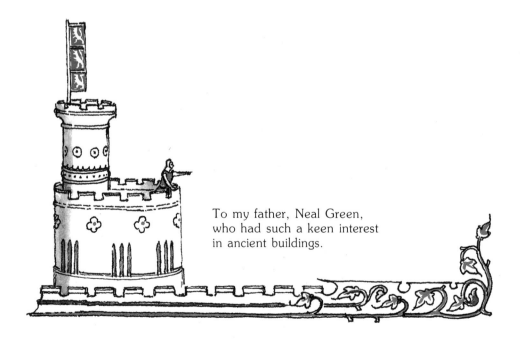

To my father, Neal Green,
who had such a keen interest
in ancient buildings.

ACKNOWLEDGEMENTS

The text and illustrations for this work are based on a wide variety of sources: the existing ruins, the writings of the medieval chroniclers, manuscript drawings and archaeological books and reports. I started my research with the *Official Guide* to Lincoln Castle; *Lincoln Castle in the Middle Ages,* by Helen Elliott, illustrated by Tig Sutton, F.L.A.R.E. 1980; *Lincoln the Archaeology of an Historic City,* by Christina Colyer, Lincoln Archaeological Trust 1975; and *Beneath the Stonebow Centre,* by John Wilford, illustrated by David Vale, F.L.A.R.E. 1983. For general background material I relied on *Medieval Lincoln,* by Sir Francis Hill, Cambridge University Press 1965. However, I was still baffled by many aspects of the ruins and made slow progress until Andrew White, then Keeper of Archaeology for the Lincolnshire Museums, advised me to study the Willson Collection which was in the Lincolnshire Archives Office at that time. These notes, sketches and measured drawings from the pen of E. J. Willson, the architect who restored the castle 1834-5, came as a revelation, and I must thank the Lincoln archivists for their help and the owners of the collection, The Society of Antiquaries of London, for permission to use this unique unpublished material. I then had the good fortune to encounter David Stocker, Field Officer (Monuments) for the Trust for Lincolnshire Archaeology, at work on the west gate of the castle. From his store of professional knowledge he was able to answer most of my questions and he also recommended relevant books and papers. His report on the west gate, published in *Archaeology in Lincoln 1982-3,* supplied additional information on the castle defences. Having finally gathered the material together and reduced it to the dimensions of a small book, my thanks are due to Kipper Scott of Lincolnshire County Council and Tom Baker for their support in the project. I am most grateful to those who supplied the translations from the chronicles, chiefly Eyre & Spottiswoode for permission to use excerpts from the *English Historical Documents* series and David Roffe for his translation from the Hundred Rolls, also Lincoln City Council for use of the Common Seal of the City. In conclusion, I would like to thank Elizabeth Nurser for her work in editing the text, and Douglas Lear for hand lettering the maps and plans.

The quotations in the text are from the following sources (*E.H.D.* refers to *English Historical Documents,* Eyre & Spottiswoode, London): page 7, Anglo Saxon Chronicle, Version D, *E.H.D.,* II, p. 149; page 18 Ordericus Vitalis, *Ecclesiastical History,* Bohn's Antiquarian Library, vol. 4, p. 215 (by permission of the British Library); page 19, William of Malmesbury, *The Historia Novella,* trans. by K. R. Potter, Nelson & Sons, 1955, p.48; page 20, Henry of Huntingdon, The History of the English, *E.H.D.,* II, p. 306-7; page 31, The Chronicle of Roger of Howden, *E.H.D.,* III, p.66; page 33, *Rotuli Hundredorum Temp Hen III et Ed I* (Hundred Rolls), Record Comm. 1812-18, I, p.309, trans. by David Roffe; pages 37, 39, 40, History of William the Marshal, *E.H.D.,* III, pp. 88, 89, 90; and page 42 ia a note from the Willson Collection, Society of Antiquaries of London.

Sheila Sancha.

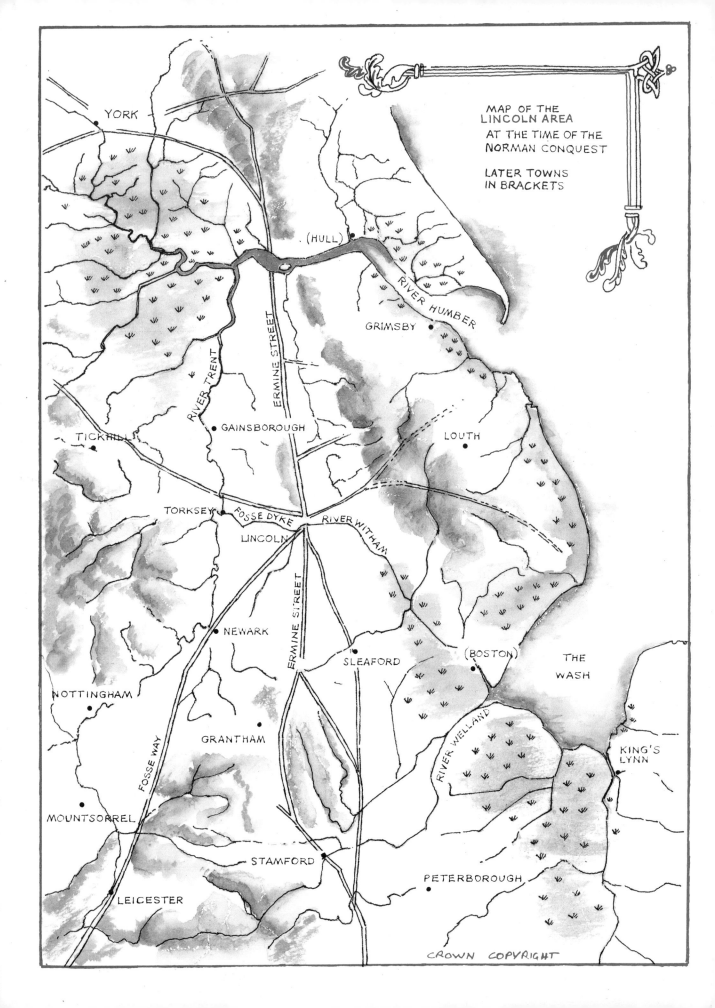

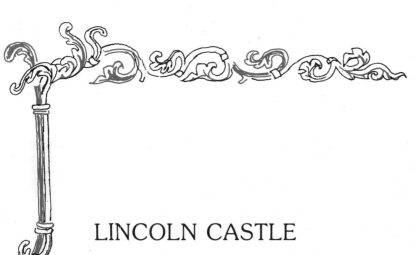

LINCOLN CASTLE

THE MEDIEVAL STORY

The Bayeux Tapestry gives a good picture of Duke William talking to his barons in Normandy. He wore a simple tunic and cloak and was aged about 39 at the time of the invasion. The Normans had short hair and shaved the back of their heads, which must have seemed strange to the long-haired Saxons.

William, Duke of Normandy, was crowned King of England on Christmas Day 1066. He had crossed the channel with a small invasion force, conquered a territory several times larger than his own dukedom, and was now faced with the problem of governing the Saxon inhabitants who bitterly resented having to obey new and foreign laws. A skilled warrior with a genius for organization, William kept his throne and control of the country by establishing a network of strong castles. The Saxons had fortified some towns, but castles were almost unknown in England at that time, whereas the Normans had been living in their individual fortresses for over a hundred years. William commanded his barons to build castles at strategic points all over England, enabling them to keep a close watch on the local communities and to protect themselves when under attack. Speed was essential, because no Norman overlord, together with his family, soldiers and servants, felt secure until they were safely surrounded by ditches, banks, timber palisades, or stone walls, if stone was available.

In 1067 William suppressed a revolt in the west country and the following spring the earls Edwin and Morcar rebelled. The Anglo-Saxon Chronicle has this to say:

> Then the king was informed that the people in the north were gathered together and meant to make a stand against him if came. He then went to Nottingham and built a castle there, and so went to York and there built two castles, and in Lincoln and everywhere in that district.

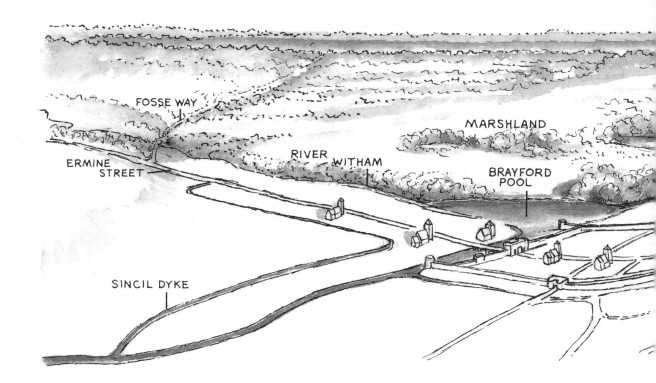

FOSSE WAY

MARSHLAND

ERMINE STREET

RIVER WITHAM

BRAYFORD POOL

SINCIL DYKE

A view of 11th century Lincoln, showing the Roman roads, canals, walls and ditches. The Saxons had built many churches in the upper and lower city and suburb of Wigford, south of the river. Goods were carried along the waterways to be unloaded in Brayford Pool, the ancient river-port that gave Lincoln its name. Llyn was the British word for lake, and colonia stood for the Roman colony.

The Normans found a ready-made site for the castle at Lincoln. In the mid-first century the Romans had built a timber fort on the crown of the precipitous hill overlooking the valley of the River Witham. By the end of the century the legions were posted away and Lincoln became a settlement for veteran soldiers, their families, dependants, and the traders supplying their needs. The status of colony was conferred upon Lincoln. The original timber defences at the top of the hill were replaced with stone walls and these were extended in the third century as far as the river, to protect the houses that had been built down the slope of the hillside. The walls and ditches were set out in a fairly symmetrical pattern. Stone towers were added at intervals behind the walls and the masonry was repaired and strengthened. In 1068 these ancient defences were still standing.

King William's men decided to use the site of the original legionary fort (the upper part of the city) as the outer bailey of the castle. Ermine Street, the great Roman road stretching from London to York, came right through the fort, entering by the south gate and leaving by the north gate, now called Newport Arch. The area was sub-divided by the road linking the east and west gates. The south-east

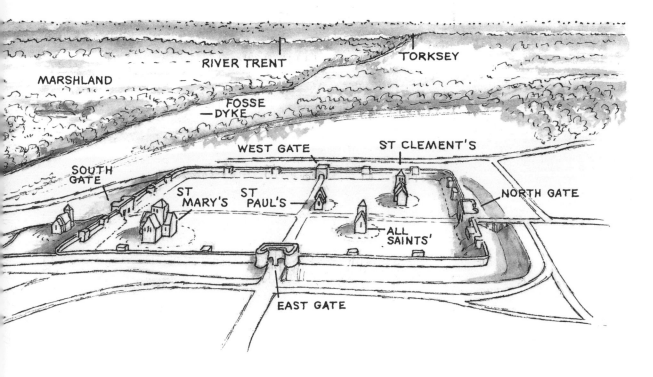

quarter was partly occupied by the Saxon Church of St Mary, although its existence can hardly be traced. St Paul's church, on the site of the Roman Forum, must be the earliest church in Lincoln: All Saints' stood to the east, and St Clement's may already have been standing to the west. The remainder of the upper city would have been crowded with small thatched timber houses, shops and stalls, with vegetable plots, herb gardens, orchards, animal pens, and sheds in the rear. Many of these buildings had been damaged by a recent fire.

Newport Arch is the inner arch of the Roman north gate, but only the top part is visible because the original Roman paving stones lie far below the level of the modern road. William I must have passed under this arch when he came to Lincoln from York in 1068.

The Normans often used Saxon labour to build their castles. Ditches were dug with spades and picks and the earth carried up the banks in baskets. 166 houses were destroyed when they cleared the ground for the inner bailey and the suburb of Newport is thought to have been founded by the dispossessed families.

It was usual for castles to have an inner and an outer bailey and the important buildings, which included the lord's hall, chambers and chapel, were placed in the inner bailey, which was better defended. If the castle was in a town, then there were often pre-existing houses and sheds filling the space in the outer bailey. The upper city of Lincoln — the outer bailey — came under castle jurisdiction and it is thought that some members of the garrison had their houses in the north-west quarter, with St Clement's (known to be standing in the twelfth century) as their own particular church. A postern doorway inserted in the north wall of the castle at a later date supports this view. The obvious site for the inner bailey was the south-west quarter, at the edge of the hill, where sentries could watch the surrounding countryside and mark the movements of traffic along the roads and rivers. In medieval times therefore, Lincoln Castle, with its inner and outer baileys, referred to the whole area of the upper city; but the outer bailey ceased to be administered from the castle in 1327 and from that year to this Lincoln Castle refers to the inner bailey alone.

The castle builders were nervous and in a hurry. The ancient Roman walls were considered strong enough to serve the outer bailey; but the vital south-west stretch defending the inner bailey must have been in a bad state and the Normans covered it with an earth bank. The massive Roman west gate was probably also a ruin and it was either buried at this time, or had been buried at an earlier period, and remained at the core of a huge earth mound. When the mound was partly demolished in 1836, the upper stones of the Roman gatehouse were discovered. The mound has raised the level of the bank at this north-west angle and it is considerably higher than elsewhere.

A new gate for the townspeople was inserted in the wall on one side of the mound, and a separate entrance to the inner bailey at the other. Two great banks and ditches were dug to create the northern and eastern defences of the inner bailey, which was now completely isolated by these immense earthworks. The garrison could never trust the citizens living in their outer bailey and if the east gate was suddenly blocked by a hostile force, they could come out of the west gate, which gave access to open country.

Lincoln Castle may have had two eleventh century mottes, if the mound over the Roman west gate is taken into consideration; but if this was indeed the original motte of 1068, it was soon discarded when they constructed the great earth mound overlooking the south-west corner of the ruined Roman wall. This motte was made of earth packed down with layers of stone and was isolated from the inner bailey by a deep ditch. There was no bank and ditch south of the motte and the people in the town below had an uninterrupted view of the great mound rising above to remind them of their Norman overlords. Before the cathedral was built, the silhouette of the castle dominated the skyline.

As with most early Norman strongholds, Lincoln was a motte and bailey castle: the garrison resorting to the defences at the motte top when the outer and inner bailies were about to be taken. The motte was placed at the edge of the bailey to give the defenders an ultimate chance of escape.

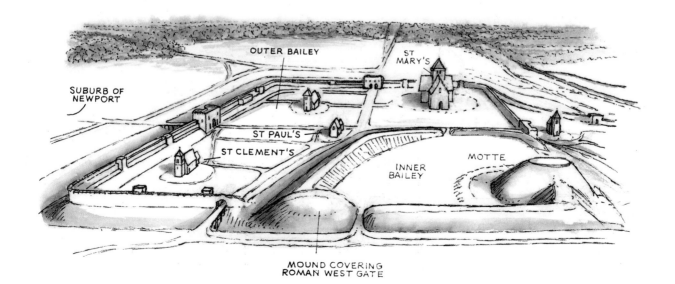

SUBURB OF NEWPORT

OUTER BAILEY

ST MARY'S

ST PAUL'S

ST CLEMENT'S

INNER BAILEY

MOTTE

MOUND COVERING ROMAN WEST GATE

Thorold the sheriff would have worn a long gown, as befitted the dignity of his office, when presiding at the shire courts; with the long Saxon hair and forked beard. It is doubtful if the sheriff had his own hall in the castle, but there would have been accommodation for his clerks and officials.
Opposite. Swein, the constable, with soldiers of the garrison.

The cathedral replaced the Saxon church of St Mary, due east of the castle. Begun in 1072, it was consecrated twenty years later, and the two great establishments of church and state faced each other across the main thoroughfare of Ermine Street, which eventually became known as Bailgate (gate being the Danish name for road).

Lincoln being a royal castle, King William I appointed a constable to command the garrison, which was partly made up from his own men and partly by the men of the bishop. Because Lincoln was the chief city of the county and a thriving trading centre, the sheriff of Lincolnshire would have held the shire courts in the inner bailey of the castle, where judgements were given and taxes collected. The Domesday Survey of 1086 lists a man called Thorold as sheriff and Swein as the first constable: they were probably both Saxons, but William's initial policy had been to select respected local officials, a policy he was later to change. Thorold and Swein were wealthy landowners and were probably both in office in 1070 when the Danish king Swein sailed up the Humber and sparked off the rebellion of Hereward the Wake, centred in the fens. In retaliation William ordered hostages to be taken from all over Lindsey and held in the castle. There are no archaeological remains or records to indicate the kind of buildings in which the hostages were held.

The shape of the outer banks and the large motte are the only certain features of the eleventh century castle, and all the interior buildings have to be imagined. There would have been a timber hall for the constable and his household together with his chamber, chapel and store rooms, as well as lodgings for his men and stables for the horses. There were the usual workshops, armourers' sheds, smithies, brewhouses, bakehouses, and all the necessary buildings serving a large community. A castle had to be self-supporting to withstand a siege. Water must have been a serious problem at this high level. One well has been located, but there would have been several.

Fresh earth cannot support the weight of stone walls and the banks of the first castle were surmounted by a stout palisade of split tree trunks. The years passed. William I died. William II was killed in a hunting accident, and the next king was Henry I. The earth banks had hardened by this time and it appears that the timber palisades were partly replaced by stretches of stone wall after a bad fire in 1113: the word 'murus' is used in a charter of 1115 and some early Norman herringbonework supports the theory.

This reconstruction is based entirely on the castles of the Bayeux tapestry and archaeological reports on other 11th century timber keeps. Nothing is known about the first keep in Lincoln Castle.

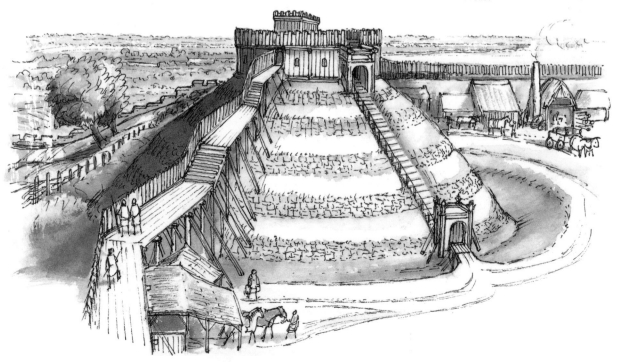

Above: The west gatehouse tower stands almost to its full height, but most of the barbican is missing.
Below: The curtain walls are made of two lines of dressed stone, with a rubble filling. There are no deep foundations and the walls were built on a framework of timber.

The two gatehouses are the oldest existing buildings in the castle and the passages would often have echoed to the clamour of mailed knights passing through. The east and west gatehouses were probably identical and, being set into the neighbouring banks with solid ground to take the weight of masonry, they could feasibly have replaced the first simple gateways before the end of the eleventh century; but an early twelfth century date is more likely. The east gatehouse was extensively altered and disguised in the fourteenth century, but it still retains the original round tunnel-vaulting over the passage. Luckily, the west gatehouse escaped a similar renovation and, although parts are missing, the main walls stand almost to their full height: a splendid example of an early Norman tower.

The west gatehouse was designed in two parts: the inner tower consisting of the tunnel-vaulted entrance passage with a room above, while the forebuilding, or barbican, was of one storey and defended the entrance. The west wall of the inner tower is still standing and the wide arch which once spanned the middle of the passage has been blocked. On either side, the massive ruinous walls of the barbican project towards the ditch and originally they would have come up to the level of the doorway giving access to the upper chamber. It is not known if the barbican was roofed over or open to the sky, but it would have had a walk-way or flat fighting platform. Archers could fire arrows from this position and men-at-arms cast down javelins, stones and other missiles. If an assault party tried to destroy the entrance doors by fire, the defenders could pour water over the parapet to put out the flames. There are similar gatehouses in the castles of Ludlow and Exeter.

Masonry foundations of an earlier building underlie the west gatehouse and these may belong to the gateway of 1086, or a very early replacement. In line with other gateways of a similar date, this entrance probably had a stone base with a timber superstructure.

The constable Swein was succeeded by his son Picot who died in 1115, after which the office passed to his son-in-law, a Norman called Robert de la Haye whose descendants were to be constables for several generations. The appointment of sheriff also seemed a family affair. Thorold had a niece, or maybe a more distant relation,

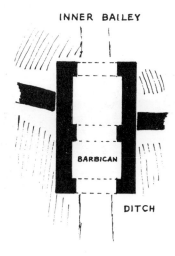

Plan of the west gatehouse in the late 11th or early 12th centuries. The curtain walls are later than the gatehouse and are not bonded into the stonework.

This photograph of the west gatehouse was taken from a position overlooking the ditch. It shows the ruined barbican walls, the blocked central arch, the two narrow loops, and the blocked doorway that linked the upper chamber to the walk-way round the top of the barbican. The ruins to the left of the barbican are of a later period.

The inside walls of the west gatehouse are either destroyed or hidden by later work. This reconstruction shows the shape of the original building, seen from the inner bailey. There is no stairway linking the entrance passage and the upper chamber, which must have had a doorway in the south wall, leading out to the top of the bank.
Below: Lucy with her first husband. Ivo Taillebois. He is called Ivo the sheriff in Domesday Book, 1086, which gives a long list of his estates. He died about 1094.

called Lucy, and she married the powerful landowner, Ivo Taillebois (pronounced tallboy), who became the next sheriff. Lucy had a lasting influence on the history of Lincoln Castle, but it is hard to get at the facts. By some accounts she was the granddaughter of Earl Leofric of Mercia and Godgifu, better known as Lady Godiva. At all events, Lucy was a great heiress in her own right and married into greater riches. Ivo Taillebois died about 1094, and the widow was contracted to a Norman baron, Roger Fitzgerald, who died in 1100, after which she married another Norman, Ranulf Meschin. The combined estates of this couple made them the greatest landowners in Lindsey, not to mention their vast territories elsewhere.

Lucy had two sons: the first by Roger Fitzgerald, called William de Roumare, and the second by Ranulf Meschin, nicknamed Ranulf 'aux Gernons' or 'de Gernons' which is either a reference to his moustache, or to a castle in Normandy. A terrible accident happened in 1120 when *The White Ship* sank in the channel off Barfleur, and the king's two legitimate sons and all their young companions were drowned. The earl of Chester was among the casualties and the inheritance passed to his cousin who was

Lucy's third husband, Ranulf Meschin: Lucy and Ranulf now became the earl and countess of Chester. On the death of Ranulf Meschin in 1129, the title passed to his son, Ranulf de Gernons. The two sons of the Countess Lucy were good friends, and they both felt they had some claim on Lincoln Castle through the right of their mother, who had once been married to Ivo Taillebois the sheriff.

The loss of *The White Ship* had far-reaching and disastrous consequences. Henry I died in 1135 with no lawful surviving son to succeed him, although he had about twenty illegitimate children, and he had bequeathed his throne to his daughter Matilda. Matilda had been the child-bride of Henry V, emperor of Germany, and after his death in 1125 she married Geoffrey of Anjou. Although Matilda was the lawful queen of England, her cousin Count Stephen of Blois crossed the channel and siezed the throne. (Both Anjou and Blois were territories in modern France.) The situation eventually resulted in civil war. Leaving her husband and infant son, the future Henry II, in Anjou, the Empress Matilda set sail for England in September 1139, accompanied by her half-brother, Earl Robert of Gloucester, and 140 knights. They landed at Arundel. Earl Robert was popular in the west country, where he held his estates, and the people gave the empress a hearty welcome: Bristol soon became their main base and rallying centre. King Stephen did his best to eject the empress's supporters from their castles and he passed the next eighteen months suppressing revolts and engaging in siege warfare. At an unknown date before Christmas 1140 the empress and her knights had succeeded in occupying the castle and city of Lincoln: this was an important achievement because at that time Lincoln was one of the richest cities in England. King Stephen hurried up with an army and forced the empress to make good her escape. These are the bare facts because the chroniclers have not left any details.

King Stephen was anxious to win the support of his powerful barons and before leaving Lincoln he 'conferred distinctions' on Lucy's sons: the earls William de Roumare and Ranulf of Chester, but the chronicler does not explain

Above: Lucy's second husband, Roger Fitzgerald, son of Roger the steward, who contributed 40 ships to the invasion fleet of 1066. He had estates at Roumare, a district in Normandy, south of Rouen.

Below: Lucy's third husband, Ranulf Meschin (the young), in the west gatehouse. He died 1129.

Above: The two countesses chatting to the constable's wife in the castle keep. William of Roumare had married a daughter of Richard de Redvers, while Ranulf of Chester's wife was the daughter of Robert of Gloucester.
Below: Ranulf of Chester and three of his men.

the nature of these favours. At this time the constable of the castle was either Robert de la Haye, or his son Richard. The garrison consisted partly of the constable's men and partly of the men of Bishop Alexander The Magnificent, who not only repaired and embellished the cathedral, but built the two episcopal castles at Sleaford and Newark. This displeased the king who objected to subject's owning castles more splendid than his own. The bishop was imprisoned and threatened with starvation until he surrendered his castles as the price of his release.

The earls William de Roumare and Ranulf of Chester were not to be bought by the king's favours and Ordericus Vitalis describes their activities after Stephen left Lincoln:

> Cautiously choosing a time when the garrison of the tower were dispersed abroad and engaged in sports, they sent their wives before them to the castle, under pretence of their taking some amusement. While, however, the two countesses stayed there talking and joking with the wife of the knight whose duty it was to defend the tower, the earl of Chester came in, without his armour or even his mantle, apparently to fetch back his wife, attended by three soldiers, no one suspecting any fraud. Having thus gained an entrance, they quickly laid hold of the bars and such weapons as were at hand, and forcibly ejected the king's guard.

They then let in Earl William and his men-at-arms, as it had been planned before, and in this way the two brothers got possession of the tower and the whole city.

During her short occupation, the empress would have provisioned the castle against the threat of a siege, the store rooms being filled with goods commandeered from shops, market stalls, and private houses: actions that might well have antagonized the citizens. When they saw the two earls had taken possession of the castle, the burgesses lost no time in sending word to the king and, despite his recent imprisonment, Bishop Alexander felt it his duty to do the same. The king's response was immediate and summoning his forces, he suddenly arrived in Lincoln one night and surprised and captured some of the earls' men who were sleeping in the city, outside the safety of the castle.

Earl Ranulf of Chester had married the daughter of Robert earl of Gloucester at some time in the reign of Henry I, and she was with him in the castle, being besieged by the king's men. Although completely surrounded, Ranulf managed to escape from a secret postern, slipped past the guards, and rode right across England to Gloucester to appeal to his father-in-law for help. Earl Robert was not the man to leave his daughter in distress without coming to her aid. Summoning the knights who had accompanied him to England, and calling together all disaffected barons whose lands had been taken by the king, or who had otherwise suffered under Stephen's rule, he led his army in a north-easterly direction towards Lincoln. Meanwhile Earl Ranulf had collected reinforcements from his Chester territories and the two armies met somewhere along the road. On 2 February 1141 they halted on the banks of the River Trent: rain had been falling in torrents and the ford was in flood. Undaunted by the swirling waters, Earl Robert declared 'he would die or be captured if he did not win the victory. Then, as all filled him with good hope, he resolved to risk battle at once, and, strange to hear, swam across the racing current of the river mentioned above with all his men.' This account is by William of Malmesbury, but a more detailed description

By some accounts the Empress Matilda was a tactless and domineering woman, but she had all the courage of her father, Henry I. She was aged 37 when she came to Lincoln in 1140 and she is seen here in her coronation costume.

The battle of 1141 was fought on the level ground, west of the castle and also raged up and down the hillside. King Stephen stood firm among his dismounted loyal knights, but his faithless cavalry turned tail and fled.

of the battle comes from Henry of Huntingdon who was archdeacon of Lincoln at the time:

> After the intrepid earl [Ranulf of Chester] had successfully crossed a marsh which was almost impassable, the very same day he attacked the king with his troops drawn up in battle array. He himself had set the first line in order, which consisted of his own retainers; the second was led by the man whom King Stephen had disinherited [William de Roumare, who had been created earl of Lincoln, but deprived of custody of the castle], while Robert, the great earl, commanded the third. On the flanks of the army were placed bands of Welshmen, greater in courage than in knowledge of arms. [Then followed two speeches delivered by the earls Ranulf of Chester and Robert of Gloucester].

> [Earl Robert] had scarcely made an end of speaking when the whole army, raising their hands to heaven with a tumultuous cry, swore not to seek refuge in flight, and, closing their ranks, advanced in arms against the foe in spendid order. In the meantime King Stephen, overwhelmed with a flood of cares, was hearing Mass with great devotion. But when, in making the accustomed offering to God worthy of a king, he was handing the wax taper to Bishop Alexander, it broke; a sign of the rupture of the king's reign. The pyx [container of the sacred bread], also, which contained the Body of the

Lord, snapped its chain and fell upon the altar
while the bishop was present: this was a token of
the king's downfall. Nevertheless, he set forth
with great energy and made his dispositions for
battle with the greatest circumspection. He
himself took up the centre position in the midst
of a host of mailed knights, who were
dismounted and drawn up in close formation.
The earls with their knights he stationed on
horseback in two lines, but this force of cavalry
appeared below strength. For these spurious
and factious earls [men who had been given
earldoms by the king to buy their support] had
brought with them few soldiers, while the king's
own army was very large and one particular
body was entrusted with the royal standard.

The earls Ranulf of Chester and Robert of Gloucester
had encouraged their armies with rousing speeches, but the
king's soft voice could not carry over the heads of the entire
army, and his words were spoken through a deputy. The
opposing armies must have been drawn up on the level
ground north-west of the castle. The disaffected barons led
by William de Roumare were in the forefront of the earls'
armies and they assaulted the king's forces with such ferocity
that the leading royalists were either slain, taken prisoner, or
put to flight. A section of the king's army then fell on the
Welshmen who were advancing up the side of the battlefield
and, being badly armed, they were completely routed; but
Ranulf of Chester came up to avenge them and scattered
the royalist cavalry, which deserted the field.

His battle-axe shattered at his feet and his sword breaking in his hand, King Stephen was finally captured.

And so King Stephen was left alone with his infantry in the midst of the enemy. The latter encircled the royal army and attacked it from all sides, as if they were assaulting a castle. Thenceforth the battle was seen to rage horribly around the royal defences, helmets and swords gleamed as they clashed, and the dreadful noise re-echoed from the hills and the walls of the city. The cavalry, furiously charging the royal column, slew some and trampled down others, while yet others were dragged away captive. No respite, no breathing-space was given, except in the quarter where the most valiant king had taken his stand and the foe recoiled from the incomparable ferocity of his counter-strokes. Perceiving this and envious of the king's glory, the earl of Chester threw himself upon him with the whole weight of his men-at-arms. Even then the lightning strokes of the king were made manifest, and, wielding his great two-handed battle-axe, he slew some and cut down others. Then a fresh shout arose and every man rushed at the king while he in turn thrust back at them all. At length his battle-axe was shattered by repeated blows, whereupon he drew his trusty sword, well worthy of a king, and with this he wrought wonders, until it too was broken. At sight of this William 'de Chesney', a very valiant knight, rushed upon him and, seizing him by the helmet, shouted with a loud voice, 'Hither, all of you, hither, I hold the king.' Everyone flew to his aid and the king was taken prisoner.

So ended the first Battle of Lincoln. The drawbridges were pulled back over the ditches, the earls retained possession of the castle, and the king was carried off to Bristol, where he was imprisoned. Lincoln enjoyed a couple of years' peace, during which time Robert of Gloucester was captured by Stephen's army, exchanged for the king, and both men were at liberty to carry on with the war. The king had another misfortune when he returned to Lincoln in 1143 and was again besieging the castle: his men were building earthworks somewhere in the vicinity of the west gatehouse, and were probably trying to tunnel under the wall, when the earth caved in and eighty of them were killed. Discouraged by this disaster, the king called off the siege. Three years later he resorted to trickery: inviting Earl Ranulf of Chester to his court at Northampton, he had him arrested and kept in prison until he surrendered the castle at Lincoln. King Stephen returned to Lincoln at Christmas 1147 for the festival and to take possession of the castle. Three times a year it was the practice of the Norman kings to summon their nobles and prelates to one of their greatest cities and enact the ceremoney of wearing their crowns. But the chroniclers talk of a strong local superstition which maintained it was extremely unlucky for a king to wear his crown in Lincoln. Nevertheless, despite his past humiliating experiences, King Stephen defied the warning and the crown-wearing took place within the city walls.

The castle was now in royal hands and it was Earl Ranulf's turn to try to get it back. He came up with an army, but the citizens would not support his cause, his trusted commander was killed outside the north gate (Newport Arch) and the attempt was abandoned. Finally in 1149 an agreement was reached between the king and the earl: Ranulf could keep the castle until certain possessions in Normandy were restored to him, and he would also be given the nearby castle of Tickhill (Yorks . Lincoln Castle would then revert to the crown with the exception of a certain tower, previously fortified by the Countess Lucy, which was to remain in Ranulf's hands.

This agreement, recorded in a charter of 1151, names two towers in the castle, but does not identify them. There may have been several stone or timber towers at the angles of the curtain walls, and gatehouses were often called towers; but it is generally understood that the tower built by the Countess Lucy was the one at the top of the great motte. This may have been a timber structure, but there is also the possibility that the existing shell-keep, the Lucy Tower, was standing before the countess died in 1136. This is an early date for the style of architecture, but without further investigation, the problem cannot be solved.

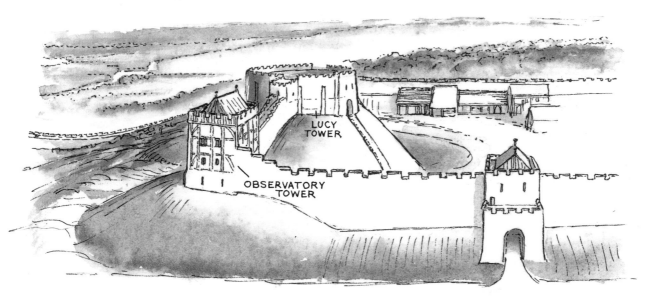

The castle was strongly fortified by the end of the 12th century, with two keeps on two mottes, when most castles only had one. The lower parts of the Lucy Tower survive, but the Observatory Tower has been extensively rebuilt. It may originally have been a timber building with stone foundations: store rooms below and hall and chamber above.

There is an equal uncertainty about the making of the south-east mound and the tower that once surmounted it. The present Observatory Tower owes its name to the high turret built by a nineteenth-century prison governor with an interest in astronomy, and the greater part of the buildings belongs either to that date or to the fourteenth century. The south-east area of floor in the Observatory Tower was excavated in 1974 and some descending steps and the walls of an earlier tower were found to underlie the present masonry, enclosing a rubble core that continued on down inside the motte. If the building was like other twelfth-century towers, the foundations would be laid at the original level of the ground and earth heaped round the tower as work progressed. Fragments of mid-to-late twelfth-century pottery picked out of the debris suggest the work of Ranulf's masons, and further excavation may confirm the theory that he built the motte and tower in the years following the charter and before his death in 1153, when the castle reverted to the crown.

At all events, the tower on the south-east mound occupied a prime defensive position overlooking the entrance to the cathedral, the Roman south gate and the busy fish market beyond. Further off lay the great spread of the lower city where the citizens were so often at odds with the sheriffs and constables of the castle.

In an emergency men-at-arms had to move quickly from one part of the castle to another and the Observatory Tower, or more rightly its predecessor, was linked to the east gatehouse by means of a gallery running through a range of buildings that stood against the south-east curtain wall. Sentries could patrol the stretch of wall between the Observatory Tower and the Lucy Tower under a covered way which protected them from enemy arrows and missiles as well as wind and rain.

A young squire descending the steps of the Observatory Tower in the late 12th century.

White areas on this plan of the Observatory Tower are 14th century or later, but the grey central wall may be late 12th century. The black areas show the top of the original Norman masonry that continues on down inside the motte. A surveyor's map of 1783 shows the tower extending further east, in line with the curtain wall.

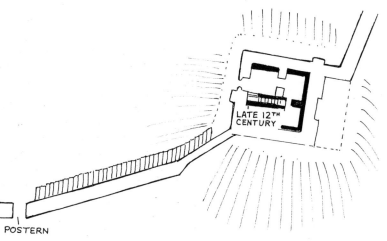

LATE 12TH CENTURY

POSTERN

The Lucy Tower is a shell-keep: the purpose of the fifteen-sided stone ring was to protect the vulnerable timber buildings that used to stand against the inner face of the one continuous wall. It is a simple structure, without the kind of architectural detail that would have made it easier to date. It certainly belongs to the twelfth century, and most authorities slot it into the period following Stephen's wars; but it could be earlier. The top of the motte, not yet excavated by archaeologists, was used as a burial ground for the later prison. The graves have disturbed the surface, but there must still be post-holes and other archaeological features to give the pattern of the interior buildings and shape of the original timber keep, down there under the grass.

It requires a great stretch of imagination to picture the keep as it was, and the best sources of information on its original form are the notes and sketches made by the surveyor E. J. Willson when he restored the castle in the early nineteenth century. Time having weathered the

Plan of the Lucy Tower, facing south. There was a vaulted chamber with a fireplace at the base of the small eastern tower, and a latrine tower to the west. The stretches of stonework connecting these two buildings to the shell-wall have been rebuilt and all traces of the original doorways have vanished, other than the great entrance arch and the south-west postern.

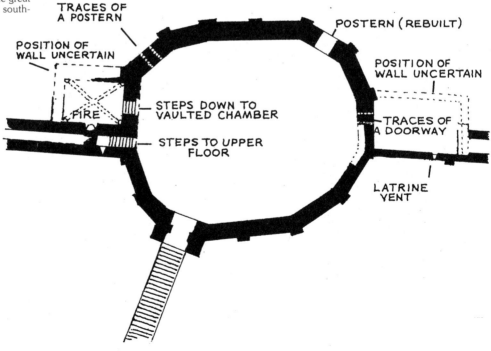

TRACES OF A POSTERN

POSITION OF WALL UNCERTAIN

POSTERN (REBUILT)

POSITION OF WALL UNCERTAIN

FIRE

STEPS DOWN TO VAULTED CHAMBER

STEPS TO UPPER FLOOR

TRACES OF A DOORWAY

LATRINE VENT

stones, it is often hard to tell which is the work of his expert masons, and which is original. The motte would have been twice as impressive when the steep slope carried on down to the bottom of the ditch that cut it off from the rest of the bailey. The original steps would have been in roughly the same position as now, approached from a drawbridge spanning the ditch. The keep was in ruins when Willson carefully restored the entrance arch, using as much of the original stonework as possible: the decoration belongs to the latter half of the twelfth century, but the Normans may well have replaced an earlier arch. There was no portcullis and the door would have been secured by slotting a stout timber beam into the draw-bar holes at the sides. Willson's plan shows two sally ports on the south curve of the wall: he blocked the east doorway, which is no longer visible, and rebuilt the arch over the west doorway. If the keep had existed before 1143, soldiers could have made a quick sortie from this postern to attack the king's men as they were digging their earthworks.

A birds-eye view of the Lucy Tower with the walls standing to their full height. The line of joist-holes give the level of the upper rooms of timber buildings that were packed round a courtyard inside the keep.

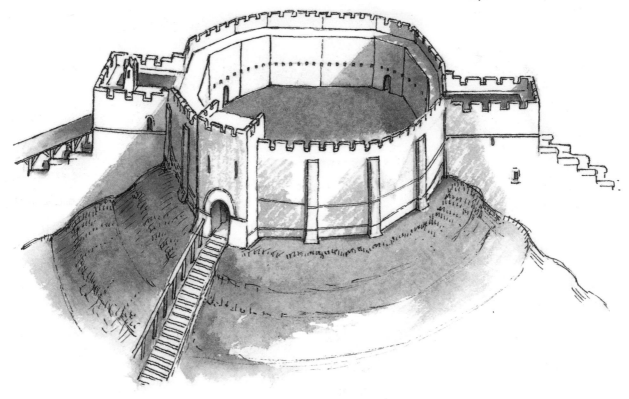

The Lucy Tower, showing the estimated height of the keep and the extent of the wall as it now stands.

The interior timber buildings were ranged round a courtyard, their beams set into the stonework of the shell-wall, the lines of brick-filled joist-holes along some stretches fixing the position of the upper floor. The twelfth-century ground level would have been slightly below the present turf. As it stands today, the keep is only tall enough to enclose the ground-floor rooms, the hall and chambers being on the floor above, and the original building would have been over double the height it is now.

There are shallow pilasters supporting the exterior of the existing stonework, but it is quite plain, without any windows which would have been a defensive hazard at this low level. There may have been openings at a safe height from the ground to light the chambers of the upper floor. Most of the rooms must have been dimly lit from windows facing the small dark inner courtyard. The service rooms would have been at ground level: probably a porter's lodge by the entrance, guard rooms, store rooms, soldiers' and servants' quarters, a kitchen, a buttery (for wine) and a pantry (for bread). The hall and numerous chambers for the constable, his household and knights, were on the upper floor. All this living accommodation was empty in peacetime, the constable inhabiting a more spacious hall down in the bailey.

The keep was the castle stronghold and place of refuge for the garrison when under attack. Barrels filled with silver pennies (the only currency), valuables, weapons, and the expensive shirts of mail would be stored in the safety of the keep. There would also be a permanent supply of stones and other missiles stacked and ready to throw over the parapet at the top of the keep if need arose. At the first sign of hostilities, emergency supplies of food and drink would be carried in. There must have been a solution to the problem of water, but there is no sign of a well at the motte top: they may have relied on a system of rainwater tanks, but this is mere speculation.

There are the remains of two towers on either side of the keep at the junctions with the curtain walls, and Willson sketched the ruins before they were altered. The western tower was the latrine block and traces of a doorway in one of his plans suggest that the building was wider than it is now. From the inner bailey a rectangular vent can be seen at the base of the tower: the rooms would have been fitted out with stone or wooden seats set over a drain which discharged through the vent down the side of the motte.

This is a reconstruction of the eastern tower of the keep, showing the postern leading to the outer bank of the motte and the two chambers, with the priest warming his hands by the fire below and praying in the chapel above.

The eastern tower was square and slightly larger, with a doorway and mural stair leading to an upper room that might have been a chapel. A separate doorway led down two or three steps to a basement room with a vaulted stone ceiling, two windows, and a fireplace with a chimney: the kind of chamber that could have been used by a chaplain.

When medieval kings visited Lincoln they seldom stayed in the castle, but lodged at some citizen's house, or at St Katherine's Priory, conveniently near the junction of Ermine Street and the Fosse Way, south of the river. This unwalled district was not considered part of the city and when Henry II came to Lincoln 1157 for the ceremony of his second crowning (Stephen having died in 1154), he took note of the old superstition and the ceremony was held outside Lincoln, in the suburb of Wigford.

There are no surviving accounts of Henry II's spending money on Lincoln Castle and his son Richard I only came to England to be crowned and to raise money for his Crusade. Richard traded anything for ready money and sold the offices of sheriff and constable to a landowner called Gerard de Camville, who had married Nicholaa, daughter of the last constable, Richard de la Haye, so keeping custody of the castle in the same ancient family.

While on Crusade, Richard had left the government of England to William Longchamps, the unpopular bishop of Ely. His pride and extravagance stirred up general discontent and when Richard's younger brother John raised a rebellion in 1191, he was supported by Gerard de Camville among the other Lincolnshire barons. Roger of Howden wrote:

> A serious dissension arose in England between the king's chancellor [William Longchamps] and John, earl of Mortaigne, the king's brother, relative to the castle of Lincoln, which the chancellor besieged, having expelled Gerard de Camville from the keepership and the office of sheriff of Lincoln; which former office the chancellor gave to William de Stuteville, and made him sheriff as well. But while the said chancellor was besieging the castle of Lincoln, the castle of Nottingham and the castle of Tickhill, which belonged to the king, were surrendered to earl John, who immediately sent word to the chancellor that, unless he quickly gave up the siege, he would visit him with a rod of iron. . . . Consequently, the chancellor, being alarmed at the commands of John, earl of Mortaigne, broke up the siege.

Mediators were called in to end the rebellion, William Longchamps hurriedly left England, and Gerard de Camville was reinstated as sheriff and constable on payment of a fine. The castle must have been damaged in the course of the siege and shortly afterwards £82 was spent in repairs. In 1199-1200 a further £20 was spent on a new tower and a gaol; but the tower has not been identified and there are not details of the gaol.

Fortunes changed and Gerard de Camville was well in favour in 1199 when Richard was killed and John became king. John often travelled through Lincoln and in October 1205 is recorded as staying in the castle: he was becoming increasingly unpopular and probably preferred the company of soldiers and protection of the high curtain wall to being entertained in the unfortified houses of local citizens. The king had lost his Norman territories to the French king Philip Augustus in 1204 and was prepared to fight to get them back. He tried to squeeze money from the church to finance the enterprise, but in 1208 Pope Innocent III excommunicated John and all his subjects. Threatened on

Nicholaa de la Haye with her husband, Gerard de Camville, constable of the castle, descending the steps of the Lucy Tower, followed by soldiers of the garrison.

all sides, the king altered his tactics, came to terms with Innocent III, and placed his country under the Pope's protection, so becoming his vassal. The barons were furious when they found they had been sold to the Vatican and, when John renewed his attempt to raise an army in 1214, obstinately refused to fight overseas. At Eastertime they were in open revolt, and after holding a meeting in Stamford, they soon gained possession of London. By Whitsun week a rebel party had occupied Lincoln.

Meanwhile Gerard de Camville had died and it is surprising to find that his wife, Nicholaa de la Haye, was now constable of the castle, which she loyally held for the king. A document of 1215 says she was supplied with six cross-bows and a giant cross-bow, while the castle was garrisoned by the men of Fawkes de Breauté, one of John's most trusted and experienced soldiers.

For a while the barons were more powerful than the king and Magna Carta was signed on 15 June 1215 (one of the four remaining charters can be seen in the cathedral library). Then both the Pope and the king pronounced the charter nul and void and the balance of power returned to the monarch. In desperation the barons took the extraordinary step of appealing to France for help and the country became involved in a full-scale war.

Louis of France, the eldest son of Philip Augustus, accepted the barons' offer of the English crown. He had a tenuous claim through the right of his wife Blanche of Castile, a granddaughter of Henry II. Although he sent an advance force, Louis did not cross the channel until after the winter.

King John came to Lincoln 23-17 February 1216 and a later document describes a meeting between the king and Nicholaa de la Haye which must have taken place at this time:

> . . . when King John visited Lincoln, Lady Nicholaa came out of the east gate of the castle with the keys in her hand and, meeting the king, she offered them to him as her lord. She said she was a woman of great age and had withstood many labours and anxieties in the castle and could bear such troubles no longer. King John replied to her gently, saying 'Please persevere as hitherto.' Thus she had custody of the castle during the whole life of King John.

Nicholaa remained constable of the castle until she finally retired in 1226. She died in 1230.

Above and below. King John arriving at the east gatehouse to be greeted by the constable, Nicholaa de la Haye, now an old woman.

Louis of France landed in Kent in May 1216 and soon occupied London and Winchester. With the authority of a king, he invested Gilbert de Gant with the earldom of Lincoln (Gilbert's uncle had been earl of Lincoln 1147-8, having married a niece of Ranulf de Gernons), and Gilbert, with the help of a certain Robert de Ropsley, seized Lincoln city; but they failed to take the castle which was being stoutly defended by Nicholaa de la Haye's garrison. When the rebels were joined by sympathizers from the north in August, Nicholaa bribed them to leave. The king hurried up from Stamford to the relief of the castle, but Gilbert de Gant and Robert de Ropsley did not have the courage to face him and retreated. King John's last visit to Lincoln was from 28 September to 2 October. He then rode north to Grimsby and south to King's Lynn, where he was taken ill. He died at Newark Castle on 19 October 1216.

This unusual reconstruction of a giant cross-bow, with the bowstring pulled back on the corkscrew principle, is taken from a 14th century manuscript. In most cases the bowstring was wound back on a winch. Giant cross-bows were useful when the defenders were trying to put the enemy siege weapons out of action.

The country was in grave peril at the sudden death of the king, and Louis of France would soon have occupied the empty throne if a group of John's most loyal adherents had not immediately taken control. Nine days after his father's death, on 28 October, John's nine-year-old son Henry was crowned in Gloucester Abbey by Peter des Roches, bishop of Winchester, who became the boy's tutor. The Pope offered active support through his legate Gualo. The royalist barons stood firm behind William the Marshal, the greatest soldier of his time and a man of untarnished reputation: he was given the title and responsibility of 'governor of king and kingdom'. Despite his seventy years, and having served under Henry II, Richard and John, few men would willingly face him in battle. The Marshal carried with him the goodwill of the majority of the people of England, and in this altered situation many rebel barons changed sides.

By this time London and most of the south-east districts of England were under the control of Louis and the rebel barons, while the powerful nobles of the west country and midlands held their castles for the king. Guerilla warfare in support of the royalist cause was carried out in the Weald of Kent, and Dover Castle stoutly held out against the French who were investing it in a prolonged siege. Activity tended to die down in the winter: Louis retired to France, returning in April 1217 to open the spring offensive. The French were still outside Dover Castle, but meanwhile a royalist force under Ranulf de Blundeville, the richest noble in England and a direct grandson of Ranulf de Gernons, was attacking the rebel garrison of Mountsorrel Castle (Leicestershire). An impetuous party of French knights under the command of the young Count de Perche rode across country from Dover to the relief of Mountsorrel, but when they arrived, the siege had been lifted. Meanwhile Gilbert de Gant and Robert de Ropsley had returned to Lincoln and renewed their attack on the castle. When they heard that the Count de Perche was in the vicinity, they invited him to bring up his knights and join forces with them against Nicholaa de la Haye and her garrison, still stoutly defending their stronghold and presumably making good use of their cross-bows and the giant cross-bow.

These stirring events led to the second great battle of Lincoln. On hearing that the French army was divided and weakened, being partly at Dover and partly at Lincoln, the Marshal and the legate Gualo siezed their opportunity. All royalist barons were summoned to a muster at Newark on Whit Monday 15 May. The legate solemnly excommunicated Louis, his entire army — including the men attacking Lincoln Castle — and all the inhabitants of the rebel city. The legate then retired to the safety of Nottingham Castle, which was held for the boy king. Ignoring the direct route up

In time of war, timber hoarding was set up round the top of the curtain walls to overhang the ditch. Defenders could climb through the gaps in the parapet, fire their cross-bows, and drop stones and other missiles on enemy soldiers as they tried to hack a way through the base of the wall. Water could be poured down to extinguish any fires that were lit. Willson noticed holes and slots in the parapet of the north curtain wall, suggesting that the hoarding was roofed over along this stretch, as seen below.

Heraldry was introduced shortly before this time and earls had standard-bearers to carry their banners. The arms of Ranulf de Blundeville were "azure, three garbs or" (three gold wheatsheafs on a blue ground). The arms of William Marshal were "party per pale or and vert a lion rampant or" (gold lion on a ground of green and yellow). The arms of William Longespée were "azure six lions rampant or" (six gold lions on a blue ground). The arms of Peter des Roches were probably "gules, three roaches naiant in pale argent" (three silver roach on a red ground).

the Fosse Way, the Marshal led his army to Torksey and approached Lincoln from the north-west in order to take advantage of the high ground up by the castle, and to avoid the enemy entrenched in the city below. They arrived on Saturday morning 20 May 1217.

There are several conflicting accounts of the battle, but the sequence of events appears to have been as follows. The royalist army was arrayed on the flat piece of land to the north-west of the castle in four divisions: the first commanded by Ranulf de Blundeville, earl of Chester, and the second by William the Marshal and his sons. William, the elder son, had formerly belonged to the rebel party, as had William Longespée, the natural son of Henry II and 'Fair Rosamund', who commanded the third division. The fourth division was led by Peter des Roches, the warlike bishop of Winchester.

From their position low down in the city, the rebel leaders could not assess the size of the army confronting them on the hill, and two Englishmen, Saar de Quincy and Robert Fitzwalter, went out to reconnoitre. They returned to report that the royalist army was outnumbered by their own men and there was therefore a good chance of winning a battle. This was sound advice. Records give 611 knights and 1,000 foot-soldiers to the rebels, and 406 knights and

317 cross-bowmen to the royalists. However the Count de Perche, being French, had no confidence in English judgment and went out to see for himself. He not only counted the knights' banners, but also the great car-standards fluttering over the baggage waggons, and reckoned an army of double the size. Convinced he was outnumbered, he refused to risk battle in the open and told his men to barricade themselves behind the city walls.

William the Marshal first sent his nephew John Marshal to make contact with the besieged garrison, and he had no difficulty in getting into the castle, but was attacked by the enemy on his return and escaped unhurt. Encouraged by this success, Peter des Roches, who knew Lincoln well having once been an official of the cathedral, approached the castle with an escort of cross-bowmen, ordered them to wait, and entered the fortress with only a serjeant. The History of William the Marshal recounts:

> He saw the walls and the houses knocked down by the trebuchets. People begged him to take shelter because the mangonels and trebuchets which were destroying everything in the vicinity, and he went in to the tower, where he found the

Trebuchets and mangonels were stone-throwing machines. Trebuchets worked on a system of counterweights and were made in all sizes. Mangonels were powered by tightly twisted skeins of rope, hair, etc.: on the release of a catch, the skein suddenly untwisted causing the beam to spring up and eject the stone.

Fawkes de Breauté's men loosing their shower of cross-bow bolts from timber hoarding on the east side of the castle. The drawbridge was probably still a loose section of the bridge that was hauled back into the gatehouse passage by hand. It would have been replaced when Fawkes made his sortie.

noble lady to whom the castle belonged and who was defending it as best she could. The lady was greatly delighted by the arrival of the bishop, who reassured her by the news he gave her. The bishop did not stop there long; he went out on foot by a postern into the town and as he was examining it, he noticed an old gate that had allowed communication between the castle and the town, but which had been walled up in former days. He had it knocked down to give entry to the host.

The gate cannot be identified, but it must surely have been somewhere near the south-west angle of the curtain wall, which has been extensively rebuilt. The Marshal seemed unwilling to lead his force through this unexpected outlet between castle and city, but it was probably used by Peter des Roches and his men.

Redoubling their efforts, the rebels continued to hurl rocks from their war machines. Fawkes de Breauté then reinforced the castle garrison with a strong body of cross-bowmen and they returned a shower of bolts at the enemy host massed in the open space between the castle ditch and the west door of the cathedral. Fawkes made a courageous sortie from the east gatehouse, was captured, rescued by his own knights, and finally returned to the safety of the castle.

Meanwhile the Marshal and his sons had fought their way through Newport Arch, the north gate of the city, and were driving the rebels back along Bailgate towards the castle and cathedral. The Marshal 'looked the finest of them all and as light as a bird . . . he carved his way three lances deep into the throng, scattering his adversaries and forcing them to turn tail. The bishop followed crying "Now, God help the Marshal!" ' The bitter fight continued. Robert de Ropsley

broke his lance against the Earl of Salisbury [William Longespée] but the Marshal dealt him such a blow between the shoulders that he almost unseated him. Robert let himself slide from his horse and went off to hide . . . . The Count of Perche performed many a feat. The Marshal saw that the French were drawing back their men from the top to the foot of the hill; he advanced upon the count and seized his horse by its bridle. But by this time he was already mortally wounded by the blow from a lance with which sir Reginald Crok had struck him through the eye-hold of his helm. In spite of this he took his sword in both hands and with it aimed three blows at the Marshal whose helm carried the marks of them. But immediately afterwards, he swayed and fell from his horse. When the Marshal saw him fall, he thought he had simply lost consciousness and ordered William de Montigny to take off his helm. When this was done, they saw that he was dead. It was grievous that he should die in this way.

Sir Reginald Crok, the young Count de Perche (mortally wounded in the eyes) and William the Marshal.

The standard-bearer of the younger William Marshal accidentally riding his horse over the parapet of High Bridge.

The French, getting the worst of the battle, retreated back towards the town where they found reinforcements and rallied, only to be beaten back once again. They were then attacked by Ranulf de Blundeville, earl of Chester, and another fierce battle was fought on soft ground down by the river. Important knights had someone to carry their standard, and the standard-bearer of the younger William Marshal charged at such a furious pace that both horse and rider fell over the bridge into the river, but he came out unhurt. Many rebels were taken prisoner and the rest took flight down Wigford High Street.

> The street proved difficult going for them as far as the gate. There they were unfortunate. A cow had wandered on to the drawbridge and blocked the passage. The fugitives killed it but nevertheless a number of knights were captured just as though someone had handed them over. When the gate was broken down Simon de Poissy and the constable of Arras were seen in flight. All who managed to escape were so terrified that every bush seemed to them full of marshals. They stopped nowhere. This was very evident at Holland bridge, which was broken; they slaughtered their horses to make a bridge over which they passed, so eager were they to cross.

When the struggle was over, the looting began, and the royalists took a hearty vengeance on the rebel city. The event became known as the Battle of Lincoln Fair. The churches were ransacked and the terrified citizens ran for their lives. Many took to the river and one boat, overloaded with women and children, capsized and sank.

The castle had been so heavily battered by stones flung from war machines that the walls must have been badly broken. It was time for consolidation and reward. William Longespée, earl of Salisbury, raised £374 for immediate repairs and a marriage was arranged between his son William and Idonea, granddaughter of Nicholaa de la Haye. Less expensive repairs were carried out in 1218-20 and in 1224-5 a further £20 was spent on the Lucy Tower.

Accounts say that the west gatehouse was 'taken down and rebuilt', but this must be an exaggeration. Architectural evidence gives a different story: the original stone vault over the passage was removed and replaced by a wooden floor. A massive second archway was built close enough to the original arch to create a portcullis slot and the portcullis would have been slung from a winch in the chamber above. £54 6 4d was spent on these works in 1233-4. At a much later date the north wall of the barbican was extended towards the ditch and some kind of platform for a war machine, or base of a tower, was added to overlook the approach. The rest of the ruins in this area are of the nineteenth century.

The accounts do not mention another important addition to the castle defences. At some time before the middle of the thirteenth century a new tower, Cobb Hall, was built at the north-east angle of the curtain wall. The origin of the name is obscure, but it may have something to do with the distinctive horse-shoe shape with its semi-circular stonework jutting out towards the ditch and the straight wall, with central doorway, facing the bailey. There must have been a previous stone or timber tower in this important position, but if these are any foundations to prove it, they underlie the later masonry.

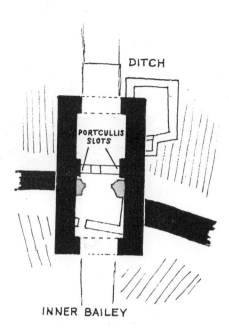

Plan of the west gatehouse in the 14th century. Black areas indicate the original building. Grey areas show the archway that was built next to the old central archway to create a portcullis slot. White areas are late medieval and modern.

The portcullis was slung from a beam in the chamber over the entrance passage and raised and lowered on a winch.

Above: Cobb Hall at its original height and with a two-light window for the upper chamber. The plans are below.

Willson left a note to say his workmen found some roughly shaped stone balls, about 250mm in diameter, when they cleared the rubbish from the posterns in 1831. He suggests that these were stored in Cobb Hall for use in one of the ancient war machines. A catapult, perhaps, or an early mortar.

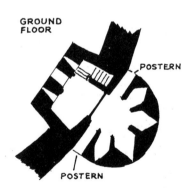

GROUND FLOOR

POSTERN

POSTERN

BASEMENT

Cobb Hall was originally one storey higher, which accounts for the present stunted look, and the upper chamber would have been used by a castle official, or perhaps an important visitor. At one time the surviving room was split in two, as Willson explains: 'The partition which used to divide this room into two parts had been taken away. It was formed of oak plants clinched together with iron spikes and had a door in it.' This suggests a small entrance lobby, lit by the two narrow windows, and with the straight mural stair giving access to the upper room (it now leads to the roof). The semi-circular area beyond the partition would have been used by cross-bowmen in wartime. The vaulting was cleverly contrived to create four deep recesses where men could stand and take aim through the long arrow-slits overlooking the approach road bordering the ditch. There were two posterns at the junctions with the curtain wall in case the defenders needed to leap out and make a surprise sortie: the facility that would have been useful in the battle of 1217. The tower basement was reached (as now) by means of a trap door and ladder, and three more recesses with arrow-loops alternate with those above to give a continuous line of fire. The proximity of the posterns being a security risk, it is unlikely that the base of the tower was ever designed as a prison, although it was certainly used as such in later times, and its use was essentially defensive. With a stone vault to the upper chamber, the building may have been firm enough to take a war machine mounted on the roof, where the commanding view included the battle site outside the east gatehouse. As it happened, this new addition to the defences was never put to the test.

A cross-bowman descending the ladder to the basement.

This section of Cobb Hall demonstrates the vaulting system of the basement and ground-floor rooms, while the timber partition has been omitted to get a glimpse of the stairs leading to the upper chamber (now the roof). There is no information on this vanished upper chamber, shown here without vaulting, and it may also have been partitioned off.

43

A carriage entering the east gatehouse in the 14th century. Doorways at the base of the stair-turrets indicate the height of the barbican wall, and the foundations of the southern drum turret can be seen in the modern car park.

Ever since the battle of 1217 the castle had remained in royal hands under the command of earls, sheriffs, and constables. Ranulf de Blundeville, earl of Chester, had been created earl of Lincoln in 1217, but resigned in favour of his sister Hawise before his death in 1232. Hawise's daughter married John de Lacy who then became earl of Lincoln. When he died in 1240, his son Edmund inherited the earldom, and it passed on to the eldest son Henry de Lacy after Edmund's death in 1258. The names of the constables are unrecorded, and the office of sheriff had lost its importance, new sheriffs being elected every few years, while there were often two sheriffs serving at the same time. William Longespée himself had been sheriff from 1217-22, but it was probably an honorary appointment, being always in partnership with another man. William Longespée's son, who married Idonea, had a granddaughter who married Henry de Lacy, thus uniting the families of Longespée, de la Haye and Lacy, and so the earldom of Lincoln still remained with the descendants of Ranulf de Gernons and his mother the Countess Lucy.

Margaret and Henry de Lacy died in 1310 and 1311 respectively and their daughter Alice married Thomas of Lancaster who actively opposed the rule of Edward II and was beheaded in 1322. The earldom then passed to Thomas's brother, Henry 'Wryneck' of Lancaster, and descended to his son, another Henry: a brilliant soldier who became the first duke of Lancaster. His daughter Blanche married the eldest son of Edward III, John of Gaunt, bringing the earldom of Lincoln into royal hands.

One of the Lancasters must have been responsible for up-dating the east gatehouse. Ideas on fortification had changed by the fourteenth century and the old Norman building would have been considered hopelessly old-fashioned. Castles were still being designed with the main eye for defence, but they also had to reflect the wealth and standing of the people who used them. The obsolete Norman arch was hidden by a new stone screen with a pointed Gothic arch, and the upper part of the tower was transformed by the addition of two stair turrets, called bartizans, projecting from the corners. Although these served as watch towers, the design of the crenellated parapet was decorative rather than useful. Doorways in the turrets gave access to walk-ways along the barbican walls, leading to the roofs of two drum towers flanking the outer gate. The entrance passage between these two towers was found to be inconveniently narrow in later times and the barbican was demolished in the early eighteenth century. The barbican guarded the approach to the east gatehouse from one side of the ditch to the other: if enemies got through the outer gate, they would find themselves trapped in a dark narrow space, at the mercy of the defenders standing on the high barbican wall, or fighting from the security of small guardrooms on either side.

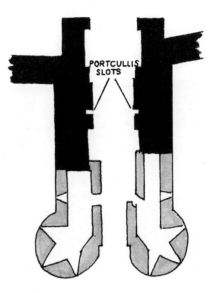

GROUND LEVEL

These plans of the east gatehouse are based on Willson's drawings. Black areas show the extent of the original Norman building and grey areas are 14th century additions.

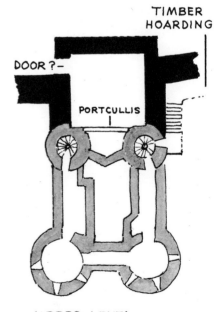

UPPER LEVEL

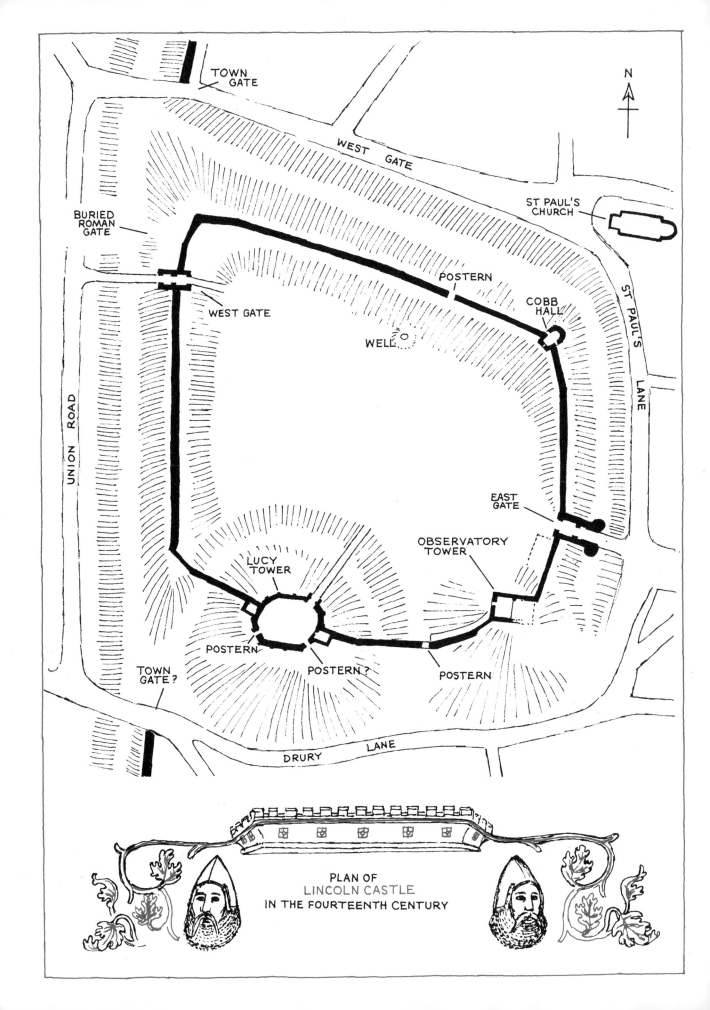

TOWN GATE

WEST GATE

N

ST PAUL'S CHURCH

BURIED ROMAN GATE

POSTERN

COBB HALL

WEST GATE

WELL

ST PAUL'S LANE

UNION ROAD

EAST GATE

LUCY TOWER

OBSERVATORY TOWER

POSTERN

TOWN GATE ?

POSTERN ?

POSTERN

POSTERN

DRURY LANE

PLAN OF
LINCOLN CASTLE
IN THE FOURTEENTH CENTURY

The rear part of the gatehouse has been almost entirely obliterated by the existing buildings which relate to the prison of a later age. Apart from the additions to the east face, the original Norman building was probably kept as it was: a simple passage with a chamber above. As with the treatment of the west gatehouse, a pier had been added in the thirteenth century to create a portcullis slot, and the portcullis would have been slung from the upper chamber. This room must have been entered from the gallery in the range of buildings that stood between the gatehouse and the Observatory Tower, because there is no sign of a stairway rising from the entrance passage to the room above.

All in all, some £500 had been spent on Lincoln Castle, after which the authorities seem to have lost interest. No more battles were fought in the town until it was captured by parliamentary forces in 1644, and the brickwork blocking the joist holes in the Lucy Tower are thought to be the work of Cromwell's men.

Sheriff's courts continued to be held in the County Hall of the inner bailey, and the king's law administered, and felons punished; but the walls, towers, and gates, which had been of such vital importance in the early days, were allowed to fall into disrepair. Frost split the stones, walls fell down, and the beams rotted. Lead was stripped from the roofs and the local builders discovered that the crumbling buildings were an easy source of well-cut stone.

Above: A blocked doorway on the north side of the north turret gave access to the hoarding on the nearby stretch of wall. Below: Reconstruction of the east gatehouse showing the narrow entrance through the barbican and portcullis hanging in place. No information is available on the numbers of doors.

BLOCKED DOORWAY

PORTCULLIS

ADJACENT BUILDINGS

This beautiful late medieval oriel window overlooking the passage of the modern gateway has no historical connection with the castle, but was taken from a house in Wigford.

An official report of 1327, the year Edward III ascended the throne, gives an interesting account of the state of the castle. The Lucy Tower had been a ruin for as long as anyone could remember; the West Tower (west gatehouse?) had fallen some time before Henry de Lacy died in 1311, while a tower called 'arountour' (Cobb Hall?) had come down before Thomas, earl of Lancaster, was beheaded in 1322. A great hall, brewhouse, stable, horse-mill and other unspecified buildings were derelict, and the curtain wall and gates would cost more money to repair than the crown was willing to pay. At a time when new castles were still being built and others enlarged and strengthened, the story of Lincoln Castle was over, and it was formally declared indefensible. The upper city, which had been the original outer bailey, came under a separate administration, and the territory of the castle was reduced to the inner bailey alone. In a later century, the ditches were filled in to create housing plots which were sold off to raise money for Charles I. When Samuel Buck made his engravings in 1726, he saw Lincoln Castle as a romantic ruin: the upper part of the Lucy Tower was missing, weeds sprouted from the broken summits of the curtain walls, and there were long cracks in the masonry.

The present buildings are a puzzling mixture of medieval and nineteenth-century work, but no castles of this great age have remained intact: they have either been heavily restored, rebuilt to suit later fashions, or allowed to crumble into vague hulks of masonry standing beside half-buried foundation stones. In early medieval times Lincoln was one of the strongest royal castles in the kingdom and the two battles, particularly the Battle of Lincoln Fair, altered the course of English history. This ancient place, familiar to kings, bishops, earls, sheriffs, constables, and the men-at-arms of each succeeding garrison, is a valuable link with the people who lived well over six hundred years ago.